Presented by Kern River Valley Art Association

"IT IS THE LAND THAT GETS US..."

Edited by John Peterson and
Sandra Rose Hughes

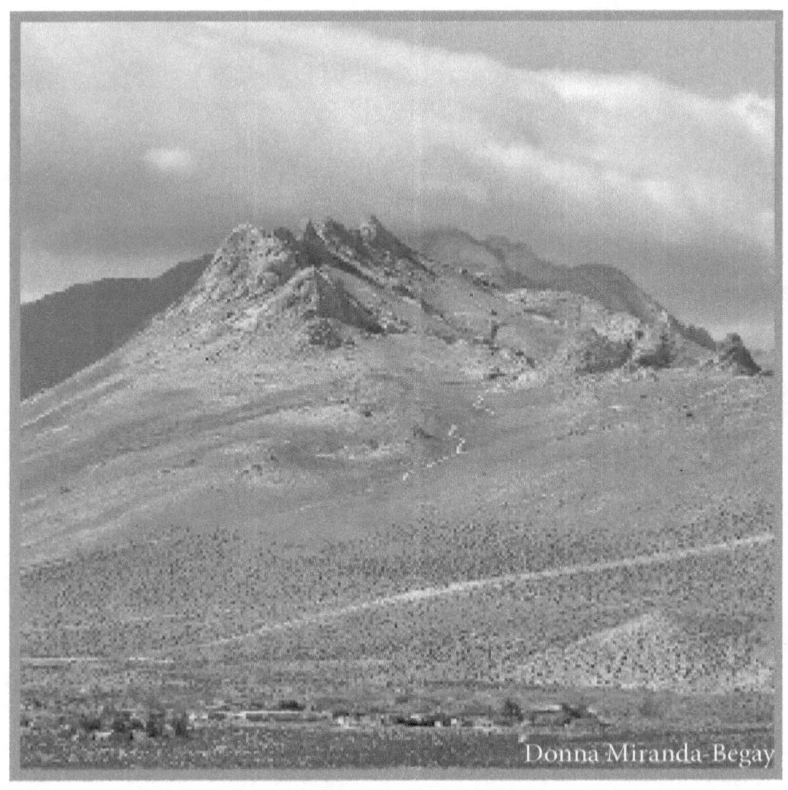

ISBN: 979-8-9896447-1-1

Published by
Poetic Matrix Press
John Peterson, Publisher
www.poeticmatrix.com

Front Cover Art
Great Blue Heron
by Joan Desmond

Back Cover Art
Tubatulabal Sun Rise
by Donna Miranda-Begay

INTRODUCTION

Buffalo Folsom ~ President Kern River Valley Art Association

This Anthology is a wonderful work inspired and produced by John Peterson and Sandra Hughes. The Kern River Valley Art Association is proud to be associated with this and delighted to have been a creative contributor. May this work inspire all of you to put pen to paper, keyboard to cloud, or brush to canvas to express feelings we all have stored inside!

Sandra Rose Hughes ~ Editor

I wanted to create this Anthology because I want good things for our valley, and I believe poetry is good for people. It offers healing, hope, humor, catharsis, and in many ways, it reveals what we really believe. I've been blown away by the honesty and courage of our local poets willing to share their work and in so doing, share a piece of their souls. I appreciate John Peterson's willingness to share his time and expertise to make this dream a reality, and I appreciate the forward-thinking spirit of the Kern River Valley Art Association.

John Peterson ~ Editor

Welcome to the first Kern River Valley Poet and Artist Anthology presented by the Kern River Valley Art Association. About a year ago Sandra Hughes began a Poetry Slam at the Art Gallery. A little later she and I began a Poetry Workshop. Out of those beginnings came this Anthology. A call was put out and these 24 poets and 7 artists with 56 poems and 12 pieces of art were chosen. A sincere thank you to the poets and artists for their submissions.

Poetic Matrix Press, started in Yosemite with James Downs, will take on the honor of publishing this work. I have told many people that my greatest joy is working with the poets and artists in producing the 100 books we have done. I can say now, once again, it has been a great joy working with the contributors to this project. Here in our Kern River Valley community we have found many fine poets and artists with something to say and the willingness to put it out to our friends and neighbors. This, along with the extraordinary Art that has been presented at the Art Gallery over many years, shows what a fine and talented community we live in.

Please enjoy this contribution to the Kern River Valley that is our home. Our creative acts are one more thing of beauty that comes from the land and its people. Sandra and I continue the monthly Open Poetry Night on the 2nd Thursday of each month at 6:00 o'clock p.m. in the KRVAA The Station.

We would love to hear your response to this effort.

Brent Puniwai - Good-Bye My Friend
—Christopher Buffalo Folsom, February 15th, 2024

As I stand and watch my friend die,
It hurts so much that he is in such pain
And knowing that he would prefer
No one should see him in this state.

In truth, if he knew, it would cause him more pain.
Our loved ones want to soothe us and let us say
Good-bye to those that we are closest.

Although we have an infinite amount of choices
In this life we really don't have much choice in how we die.

Someone else takes control, a Doctor or Nurse
Trying to relieve the pain but just making
The universe cloudy and confusing.
At this point there is no dignity or control.

I am very grateful I was able to express my love
And respect before it came to this!
I leave because of that respect for him!

Good-bye My Friend!
Our energies will blend at some point in time!

Content

Cracked Colors
Image by James Taylor

Dream House
Image by Andrina Ortiz

BEAUTY IN BROKENESS
Image *by* Michael Griffin

Run to Remember
Image by Andrina Ortiz

POET & ARTIST BIOGRAPHIES

PERSONAL NOTES

It is the Land…

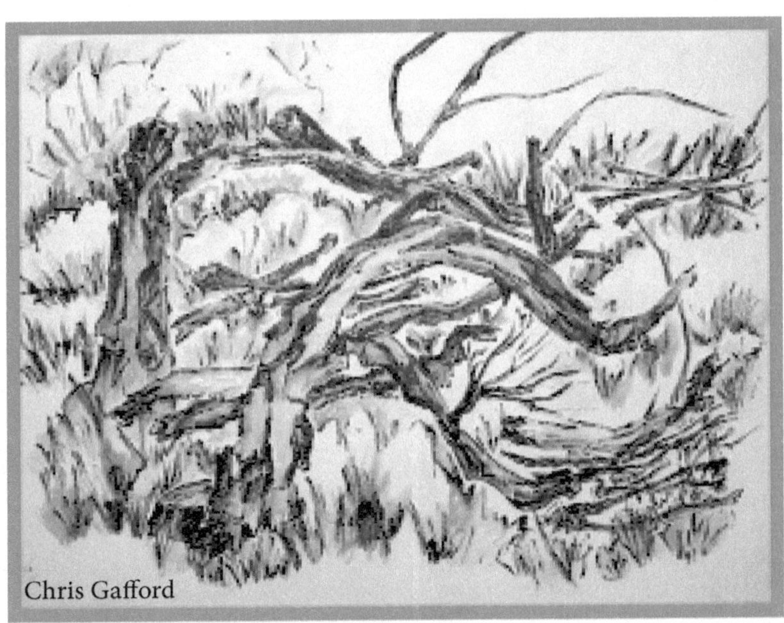

"*It is the Land that Gets Us...*"
by John Peterson

It is the land that gets us first,
this long lean Kern River Valley.

But land is too large a word,
let us speak of the mountains we see
all around this Valley.

Mountains, another large word.
You see, every mountain is its own unique expression,
no mountain is like another.

I have been to the mountains all over this country,
parts of the world: the Greenhorn Mountains here,
the Sierra Nevada, the Rocky Mountains, Great Smokies,
the Tehachapis, the mountains along the
Vietnamese Cambodian border,
the coffee covered hills of Nicaragua.
Not one is the same anywhere,
everywhere they are different,
unique in shape and size, the curves and slopes,
the rocky climb, the falling off.

As here, when we deem to see,
to let each particular see us.
Here, the granite walls riding the canyon.
That great, almost rust colored boulder,
just after you enter the canyon,
taking in the sun each day for a million years.
What do they do with this sunlight,
this heat, this cold?

1

And the plant that calls out, the gold California Poppy,
Yellow Mariposa Lily, Western Redbud.
And that Valley Oak by the river.
There is one, you know, near you, that shelters you
from the too hot summer sun,
you know it,   unlike all others.

Ah, that American Crow, yes, they all look alike
until you watch one outside your door as it catches the wind,
circling around, wings sturdy on the invisible breeze,
caw-cawing to its partner in an alien language we do not know
but indeed, they do, as they light on the power pole
or the Mulberry in my back yard,
their beauty intact.

You see, the large notion always breaks
to the gorgeous paradigm of unique expression.

The Joshua Tree further up the valley,
each character jostling with the land.
You cannot see them all, as each one makes
a startling demand on you
to look at it, see it   see Me.

This curious brain of ours wants to assign each of us
a category. We are white, black, Nancy Wilson, Julie London,
Ella Fitzgerald beautiful, with voices that   know   our   heart.

We are large small, brown or blonde, man woman,
young and old, then we say, we know you, but,
like the rocky slope, we are fooled.
Our beauty shines forth like the Joshua in the evening sun
and we must see each other,   as   we   are.

～2～

This valley fools us and soon enough
we are another of its unique expressions,
as one with the boulder and the sharp Canyon road,
the Valley Oak by the darkening indigo water

Another of that that gives its life
to the glory that is all about us.

*(Written at the request of Art Sidner for, and read at, the film showing
of Kern River Valley Horizons)*

FOR ME, IT'S THE SKY...
by Sandra Rose Hughes

It's the sky that got to me
Cast in blue as it most often is
A blue, blue, blue, bluest backdrop
For the craggy mountains.
How can there be so much blue
In all the world?
Blue in the sky,
Reflected in the lake
And in my children's eyes.

THE PRINCE OF THE SANDS
A found Poem compiled by Sandra Rose Hughes from
Badwater, a screenplay by Brent Puniwai

The Prince of the Sands rode his three-legged steed
      cross the desert
Though the desert was fraught with danger,
      the prince was fearless.
He had a date with the one and only love of his life,
      the Princess of the Sky,
And she had a silvery flying carpet
Powered by two PT6A dash 67R turboprops

The prince had already ridden a hundred miles,
But he would ride to the ends of the Earth and beyond
For an evening with the princes
…And the princess would endure a thousand tortures
To be in the arms of her prince.

Of course there was this dragon,
But the princess was fearless

Kern Valley Tale
by Catherine Stachowiak

They walked the river, without remorse,
hobbling on tiptoes the stony shores.
Pointing out all the gulls and the ducks
they giggled about their beaks and their struts.
Along the shore they ate dinner at a bench
with pastrami on pickled buns that were drenched

In moonlight they smiled about life's delights
while enjoying all of the holiday lights.

They lived by the lake, with a window view
of morning's lakeside foggy-dew.
She baked him cookies and dinner leftovers.
And at night they snuggled under warming covers.
Sometimes they walked through a park afternoons,
and they lived in their little social cocoon.

They decorated the Christmas tree
she carefully bought so happily.
He hung holiday lights very lazily.
They shared love of music, books, and TV.

The two danced on New Year's Eve alone.
They crossed a Jordan, together by stone,
one day walking, hand in hand in prayer,
knowing God would always be there.

PROMISED LAND
by Catherine Stachowiak

Would you come on my adventure,
face the Promised Land with me?
Would you come to a new future,
to the place of things to be?
Would you know it when you get there?
Would you sense that you are free?
Could you taste the fruited vine there,
how He led so faithfully?
Milk and honey waiting, pure,
as the sun rises, and fair.
Don't let stiff-necked fear keep you
from a cherished future there.

I Hike the Mountains
by Doug Schanzenbach

To spend the day
In nature's array.
I pant and heave
As up I weave
And reach the top
Before I stop.

I scan the sky
As clouds drift by
Retrieve the book,
Sign after I look,
Commune with the breeze
And listen to the trees,
Soak in the view
For a moment or two,
Soul renewed
My spirit refueled,
I snap a photo,
It's time to go.

I turn my attention
From esoteric reflection,
Cross repeated ground
Now homeward bound.
An occasional slip
I stumble and rip,
Different strength required,
The body's a bit tired,
Muscles get slammed,
Joints get jammed,
The perspective's changed
All seems rearranged—
Keep a steady pace,
Keep a steady pace.

WILDFIRE
by Joan Desmond

I
Even inside you taste soot
pushing in through cooler vents
pine, cedar, manzanita;
the mountain coyotes are burning.
How oddly this wet ashtray scent
sticks against the sky
thickens it, drags it down
taints evenings orange-gray.

II
Everywhere somewhere is sound
helicopter rotors
plunge buckets into the lake
sloshing spray, a lost and fallen thing
trails after into smoke.
Old bomber planes foam at fire
boasting warlike from their bellies
retardant stains like wound debris
fluorescent on this earth.
The screaming flames bully on
wasting everything everywhere

III
Even then inside you remember the drill
close windows to smudge and ash,
unlock doors, front and back in case.
A firefighter's grim knock echoes,
alarms the house, straightening walls
how clear still now that sharp white moment
remembering how it found you
carefully shutting the door as you left.

(Published in Metamorphosis Literary Journal, 2006 - revised)

LUNCH ALFRESCO
by Doug Schanzenbach

A picnic table
At the rim of the canyon.
The GRAND CANYON.
On a cross country trip.

Bologna and cheddar cheese, mustard,
Extra thick wheat bread.
Grapes, cut up celery, and apples.
Healthy.
Delicious.

Raven must have agreed.
As I gazed into the spectacular
Canyon depths the bird, sun gleaming
Off his black feathers, flew off with my
Top slice of brown mustard covered bread.

"AAAWK" he screamed,
Dropping the bread.
As I retrieved another slice of bread
It occurred to me: Perhaps he
Prefers Grey Poupon.

Now That I Am Old
by Magan Weid

In the land of haves and have nots lay a sleepy, small town
Where no one important knew anyone not worth knowing.
June through August weren't harsh but were kinder
      when the sun went down.
Mornings were misty and pastel sunsets were fair glowing.

Mist breached hilltops by twilight, cooling my early slumber.
Down the valley, fog crept through vineyards thick
      with mustard, and
A river running along the center in high summer
Meant loud frogs at swimming holes and living close to the land.

On long, unlit lanes, I'd walk alone to a graveyard shift.
I'd sit at my desk with windows wide open and listen
To occasional birds startled awake before they drift
Off again in silence to a steady heartbeat's rhythm.

At dawn, on clipped lawns, the wealthy dined outdoors
      with champagne.
Exciting rides in bright hot air balloons were picturesque,
Rising in chill air with blasted flames roaring like a freight train
Next to the baker's where I'd stop for fresh loaves
      and warm baguettes.

With wine and cheese amid rustling leaves near flowing water,
My breakfast was soft with bird song and torn bits
      of floured bread.
I have no loud and rousing memories: the silken flutter
Of wonders in such splendor as I have had need not be said.

(Published in Metamorphosis Literary Journal, 2006 revised.)

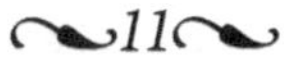

Barriers
by Maggie Giddens (12 years old)

People think they own it all.
The lush forest.
Buzzing bees.
But we fail to recognize,
The trees,
For the barriers that they are.
They are what separates civilization,
From the wild.
Once you cross that border,
There is no specific way.
No order.
Just the nighttime, and the day.
Want to come in?
The trees will block your way,
leering and sneering as if to say;
This isn't your place, now go away.
One yowl from a predator gets all the critters on their way.
Sometimes silence is the only sound,
Almost always, you will hear the mouse's nervous feet.
Like a timid little boy,
Asking for a sweet.
The lion is a confident fellow,
Yet still lazy,
And mellow.
All the creatures working tirelessly, not ceasing until their
paws, talons and flippers fall off or rot away.
Enter this place, if you dare, but be warned, beware, all the
other animals need to eat too,
And if thou enters the forest,
They might see you.

Cow Time
by Donna Miranda-Begay

Living on our Tubatulabal Miranda Tribal

allotment land is healing

Knowing our Tribal ancestors had a rough life

We continue to be strong as we live on our ancestral lands

I wonder what our ancestors would say about our today life

The birds, rabbits, squirrels, humming birds, and

snakes bring life to the land

Our allotment still sits above Kern Valley

Our allotment water continues to come from the earth

Our village is "yii-tii-en-ep"—where the flat-water lives

I see the cows coming up the hill to graze on the grass

I am a former flat lander from Sacramento

I appreciate the herd of cows that block our

allotment dirt road

This beats the big city traffic any day

As I slowly drive by these cows, they side eye me

The cows have their cycle of day and life

Up the mountain in the evening

Down the mountain in the morning

New calves come in the spring

The cows are on "cow time"

BEAR IN TRANSITION
by Donna Miranda-Begay

It was a day of harvest to gather "saat"
—Indian Mountain tea in Kern Valley
As I approach our "saat" harvest area,
I hear the wind and see the blue sky
I am near a small creek, and I see evidence of animals
and birds that live in this area
I begin to harvest the "saat" harvest area
and can hear the wind blow
The wind sounds like a song that you hum
I find myself standing amongst the granite boulders
I look down on the ground and I see bear foot prints
I look around to see if the bear is still in the area
It is late winter, the bear must be awake from its
long winter sleep
I wonder if the bear is waking up early
due to the change in our climate
I hope the bear has enough to eat and drink
I wonder what the bear looks like after a long sleep
I go home with my harvested "saat," and I start to draw
As I draw, a tune for a song comes to me
I will call this song the "saat" song
As I draw, a bear and tribal sach come to me in my drawing
I call my drawing—"Bear in Transition."

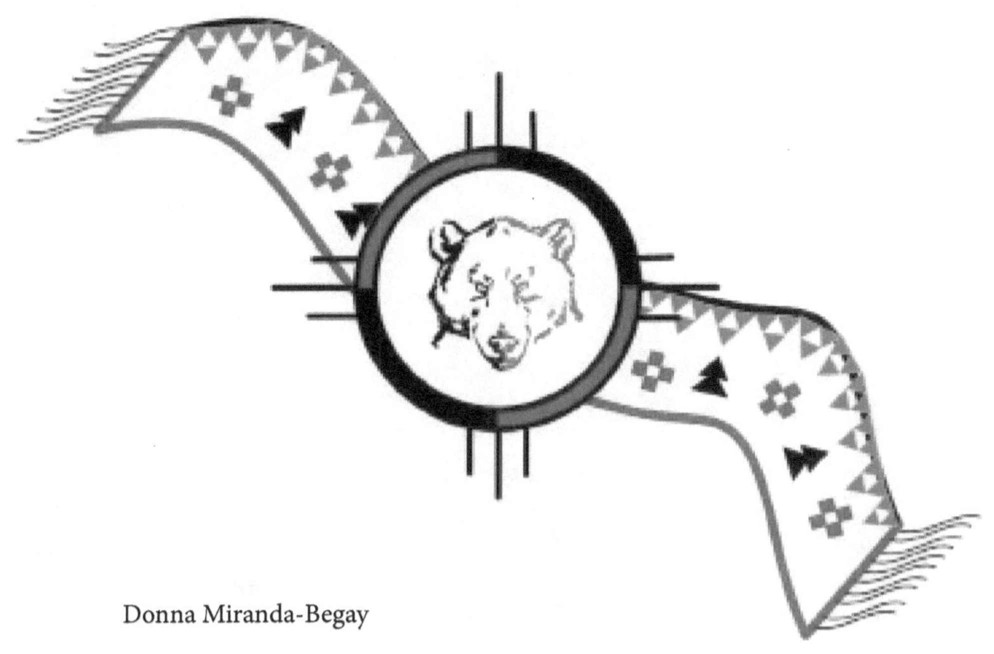

Donna Miranda-Begay

CRACKED COLORS

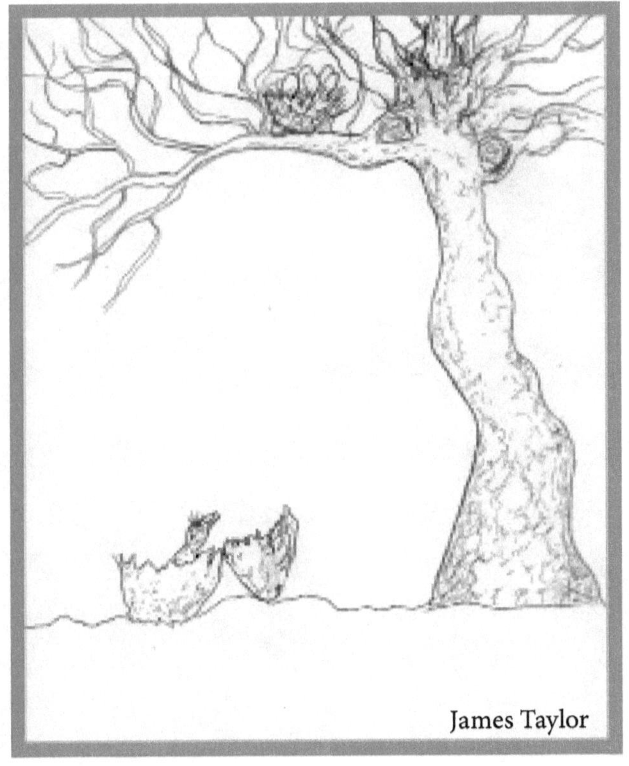

CRACKED COLOR
by James Taylor

I'm ready to go

I need a ride

the colors are cracked

but isn't the world too

I try to fit in somewhere
between the cracks
in crack of dawn perhaps
when the light is hypnotically tranquil

there must be a place that's right
a place to squeeze into
like entering a tiny diner
there's room for one more in the corner
as I try to fulfill a hungry dream
the colorful cook whips up a dish
just for me a beta carotene salad
and a glass of carrot juice
please turn on that vintage neon sign
I love to see the colors wave at me
as I walk out orange

cozy as a creature
that maneuvered down between the roots
hoping to surface once again in a world of color
the world is an abstract painting
but it thinks it's real

My Rainbow Friend
by Amanda Raymond

On a journey, travelin' fast
Ahead of me, my hidden past
Our destination, drawing near
Inside of me, a world of fear

In the distance, sat clouds of doom
Dark and gray—no sun, no moon
The storm approaching promised rage
Warning me of coming days
Lightning filled the sky with light
Rain poured down, with all its might
Now and then the sun broke through
Painting streams of nature's hues
On went the war between sun & storm
Asking me—"why were you born?"

My soul, my heart, can feel no more
Because I loved, I learned the score
I trusted you, but now I see
That one plus one can't equal three
The childhood dreams
The grown-up pain
Too much deceit
I have no name

As I draw near to my home-front storm
I hold my breath, I feel so torn
To face the truth, as I must do
Reveals to me a whole new you

You tried to make my life a lie
But now I know that I can try
To see that sunshine through the clouds
To find my name, and shout it loud

That peace seems very far away
But I'll hold dear that rainy day
For through the sun and clouds and rain
I asked the Lord to keep me sane
And then I asked Him for a sign
A miracle, that was just mine
I gazed out to that stormy sky
And saw a rainbow, way up high
The colors were glowing as if heavenly lit
Then a second one appeared beside it
"This is my sign," I said to myself
No man could buy it—"whatever his wealth
And so when my journey was nearing its end
I had in my heart, my rainbow friend
So life will go on and the pain goes on too
But I found with each raindrop and beautiful hue
That I am OK, no matter what comes to be
'Cause in each of those rainbows was love, just for me

AUTUMN AFTERNOONS IN REDWOODS
by Magan Weid

Bright sun streaks down halls of tall branches.

Glyphs and letters like fine dust glitters,

Flicker mid-air like random glances.

Sometimes in words that briefly shimmer,

But quietly sink into jumbles.

Noises escape like gases where they

Decay and send some secret message

I don't understand, then fade away.

Piles of them, now and again, quiver

With soft spoken whispers and mumbles.

"Love"
by Bill Hogarth (89 years old)

Meditation is the window to one's deepest, inner soul.
Bring to Him the many pieces; His embrace will make you whole.
Like the rays of morning sunrise, Love illuminates the way;
Guiding us along the path toward that promised, glorious day!
Love, and Love alone's the answer, to the every need of man

Strive for it; Possess it; Share it; Then you'll realize His plan.

"Vision"
by Bill Hogarth

There is so much beauty if one will only "see."
And peace that's indescribable born of tranquility.
He made it all; and gave us reign for all eternity.
A priceless promise of His love; and we have but to "see."

Vision comes not through the eyes, but from the heart and soul.
He gave to man ability, to "see" but not control.
The beauty that surrounds us as we journey through this life,
is capable of calming fears, and soothing daily strife.

Walk by a raging river or a slowly, babbling brook;
Stand 'neath a forest giant; or a canyon overlook.
Observe the springtime flowers; or the creatures that He made.
The clouds, the breeze; the summer sun; a welcome spot of shade.

If you can't see His hand of Love in everything you do;
Then you will never "see" my friend; and how I pity you!

THE DECEPTION
by Joan Desmond

Against the fading sky
the pine trees rimmed the mountains
lace-like
As if some billowing black velvet skirt
was thrown carelessly to the ground
creased and folded
into mounds and valleys
And this
which hardly merits a passing glance
in a brighter time
beckons mysteriously
against the fading sky

(Published in Orpheus Literary Journal, Fall 1999)

An Ending She'll Never See
by Maggie Giddens

A light
At the end
Of the tunnel

A Rainbow
After
The rain

But
What if it
Never comes.

What if she gives up
before
she reaches the end

What if the rain
Drowns her, and she's
Not there for the rainbow

That would make
Whatever happens next
Meaningless

All around her
Light would shine
But in her head

She's still
In the tunnel
She can't ever escape

She's dead
Breathing
But not really alive

And the world
Will go on
Without her

But I'll stay
I can't imagine
Leaving her

I suppose
That would make it
My ending too

Waving Pine Tree
by James Taylor

Looking out my window
At the rainy blustery day
The large lanky pine waves to the rain
I think it is waving at me too
it must feel refreshed after summer's drought
I'm not a tree but I think it feels the same as me
We're on this earth together

Don't blow down
Don't leave me now
As the wind accelerates
I'm hoping the wind makes you stronger
Walking against the wind strengthens my body
Building muscles through resistance
We will stay strong in our short life times

You are loaded with ripening pine cones
Ready for a squirrel harvest
Would I be a little crazy to wave back at you
Perhaps I'll just talk to you and call it a pine prayer

THE FAIRIES OF AUTUMN
by Michael Schulte

When the fairies fly from the cottonwood tree,
  and we watch the southerly migration of geese,
  and our children dress as goblins and thieves...
The nights turn colder.
Our bones feel older.
As we remember again the oncoming fall.

Behind The Waterfall
by Randy Hayes

There is a place between the mountains.
Behind a million trees.
Where fairy dust swirls.
Just above your knees.

Flowers always bloom there.
Every color you will see.
But not everyone can see them.
Only you and me.

If you take the trail at night.
And walk for one long day.
You'll come upon a waterfall.
Where the dancing fairies play.

If you listen to the fairies.
They will tell for you a story.
They will give to you a treasure map.
To a place of sweetest glory.

You will have to take another trail.
Up to the mountain base.
Where there is waterfall.
And feel the mist upon your face.

If you listen to the water.
And believe the whispers on the wind.
There behind the waters.
You will find a special friend.

When I was there I met him.
The wondrous unicorn.
He was sitting all alone.
Lonesome and forlorn.

He is the guardian of a treasure.
That the fairies made.
He offered to share it.
So for a little time I stayed.

He gave me some words to say.
Then showed the glowing well.
The wishes that I made that day.
I can never tell.

He let me ride upon his back.
All over this magic land.
He taught to me many things.
And made me understand.

The magic is eternal.
Always in my head.
And that's when I awoke.
Laying in my bed.

It had been a dream you see.
But some nights I can return.
When I miss my unicorn.
And for the magic which I yearn.

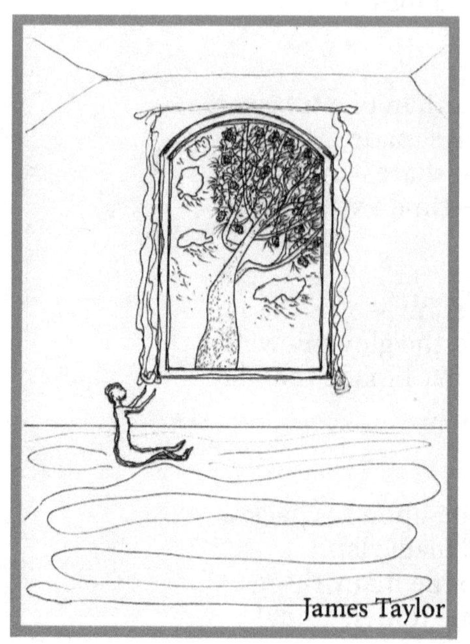

James Taylor

Dream House

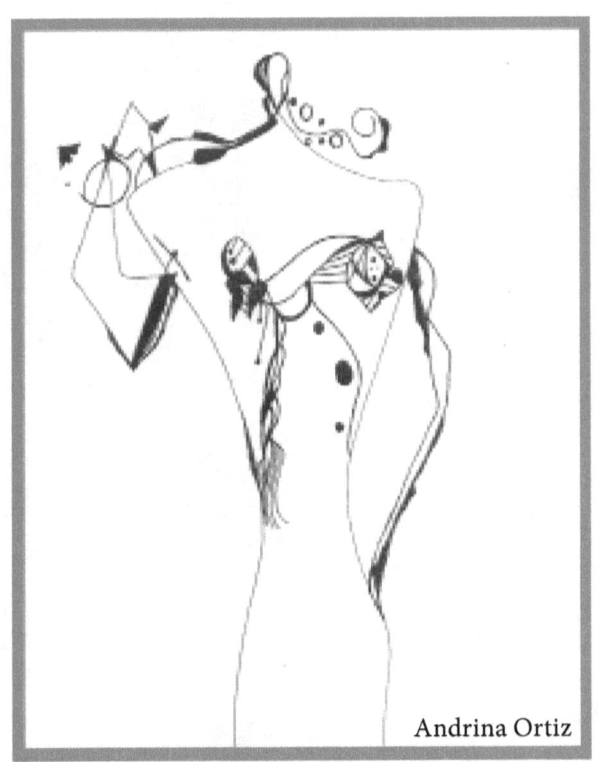

Andrina Ortiz

DREAM HOUSE
by Sandra Rose Hughes

        I roll from side to side,
my swollen belly unable to find a comfortable position.
I dream of days before the children,
Days when I swam in the early morning,
Ran, danced, sang,
Wore black leather boots on dates.

        In my house, my husband lies sleeping next to me -
Dreaming of the canyon,
of walking hip replacement patients,
Of the adventures he will take with our son,
Of mountains to climb,
Of worried ramblings—will he be able to protect us all?

        The baby sleeps in the bedroom across from us.
Perhaps he dreams of the large white dog who visited recently-
His desire to pat the creature competing with his terror of
Its gigantic size and panting tongue.

        The 6-year-old dreams that she is not asleep at all.
In the morning she will tell me that she laid awake all night
With her eyes wide open.
She is also secretly hoping I will buy her a gumball machine.

        The 8-year-old in the bunk above her rolls over,
Even in her sleep cautious of the edge.
She dreams of fights with friends,
Of cats who scratch,
Of the bracelets she makes.

The 11-year-old boy, oldest of our brood,
Sleeps deep, his dreams still undisturbed by lust or longing.
He dreams of running after his sisters,
Who he cannot find on the mountains,
Who will not answer when he yells
And will not obey him.

The new baby stirs in my belly
Kicking up and down against my skin
—dreaming of dark and light,
Sound and silence,
Warmth, constant food,
and wondering why the world seems smaller
These days,
Held as she has always been
Within my body,
And in the arms of her Creator.

Drink Me
by Sandra Rose Hughes

Where is the bottle that will make me shrink,
So I can enter by the smallest door?
Shrinking, calming, breathing, being;
Eating, drinking, resting—so much resting!
I don't wish to eat, to drink, to brew red raspberry tea,
Take my vitamins, eat dates, or take my nap.

I don't want to enter the smallness,
The tunnel, the months of stillness.
I want to burst out, break out,
Work and do, see and touch,
talk and travel—

But instead, I shrink;
A small human needs me.
Tiny people require a tiny world.
Where is the bottle that will
make me shrink,

So I can enter
by the
smallest

door?

An Escapade. Your House; Tonight.
by Avraham Baruch

A cloud fell down upon my head,
With cotton thoughts and dreams a-fizzed,
A soda pop, a cookie crack,
A wake-up call, and I am back.

It's easy to call myself,
A child adrift, on clouds-o'-nine,
But not so easy 'tis to say,
I'm sorry now, I will not stay.

A dream has gone, a-wronged alone,
A thought has come, a-wry before.
Is it I, or is it not,
I, who assumed and went along.

Your game is fine, your curtain stained,
Your thoughts were mine, for but a day.
Upon the screen a rubbered dream,
And I am gone, buh-bye my dear.

A cookie crumbled, it's morning now,
Your soda is flat, who would've thought,
The cloud just lifted; the fog is gone.
Dissipated; disappeared, 'twas for naught,

A fever-dream?
I'd say 'twas not!
But for a night, a fateful thought.
And we shall all, just carry on.

SAND
by Kimberly Salazar

Mountains,
Majestic collections of stone
Full force, the wind blows,
Unaware of its aggression
It casually roams
Invisible to all, but to my visible bones

A winter's never unearthed me so
How easily it triggers
This heavy, seeping, separating form
A stone trembling to return to sand
Numbness
The only one which understands

The only one with some consideration
Bringing relief
Like a long-sought-out savior
Determined to freeze
It's host's ever-falling precipitation

It lulls me comfortably
Into forget
Eases with compassion
The weight of regret

Here I have a cup that needs filling Held
with a hand that shivers unwilling Hoping
for a caring heart to pay heed To one
sitting beside
A construction that feeds all need

Pity we do not sprout fur upon discomfort
Pity the stomach demands daily feeding
Pity I tremble from lack of needs fulfilled

Pity these tears refuse to fall
Pity that I appear invisible to all

Pity that though eyed
These fellow creatures be,
They cannot see.

I am you,
And you are me.

SEARCHING
by Amanda Raymond

Everything is in its place
The gentle hum of a sleepy household soothes me
Life goes on around me
Yet, I am sitting in a void
Patiently waiting for words that are strangers to me
How ironic to be so full yet so empty
Maybe I'm searching too hard
The search ultimately blinds me to myself
People with empty faces and full wallets watch me
Yet, I am invisible
Only because I choose to be
In reality, words are my feeble attempt to remain human
When I stop searching, I shall awake

A Special Gift
by Lisa Watkins

I know you can't
Promise me
diamonds,
But I know
that you can
Promise to show
me the Stars!

I Hate Being Youngest
by Michael Schulte

I woke up first, before the sun.
I got up first, to jump and to run.
I ate breakfast first, then fed the cat.
I played the computer, then watched rugrats.
I went to first grade and learned in class.
I came right home...
...and then I was last.

SAM
by Michael Schulte

My birthday is coming soon...
  it's only 12 months away.
Dad says my birthday came and went...
  but that was yesterday

BRING ON THE NEW DAY
by Michael Griffin

So you're talking about Reading,
join us for the next edition.
Its about potential.
We went June
to August.
It looks like black oil and water
It was stolen but I never said it
and they think that we should
I will never forget that slow-motion look in my
mother's eyes—get married,
either way we have a story.
That body bag at the rack looks pretty
I look that way during work.
I got a plan which is interesting
A combination of flying and dying
so much so that she went to visit Kirstin
and it's like in a way not breaking up
as did I
as did he
as did she
at my brother Joe's wedding
they're taking family photos.

Like at my mother's house
you know me
you may not
doesn't matter
can we talk about this next summer?
It can be real, resembles another calamitous situation
And it's going to take years and years to fix it
but I'd like to think it won't

I started planning the wedding
that you could send me to that Island you talk about
I wasn't completely into it
But open to the idea
It was just us staring at each other with just butter on yours
And bread on mine
and us like two old biddies
criticizing the driver
then we're criticizing each other
Its toxic
so let's shoot at drinks on the house
so we can we go down to the beach
it was ugly
this very small group of guys
they were so mad at us
you know because
they're having like their dream vacation.

Those truths that destroyed their reality they were sent there
by fashion models all air brushed and everything.
And on day one of our Caribbean dream vacation
Heather had a joke but it didn't register earlier.
It was a debacle a tragic farce
When he said that's the worst place to get in an argument
We all nodded in agreement.
The whole lot of them still angry
I can't remember but is it at 10?
So you now know the answer?
Or simply horse on them
but I think it was a dangerous game to destroy another's
belief system with facts and scientific proofs.
It is much more an amorphous habit but still pretty
terrifying to those indoctrinated like so many Americans are.
Press one if you'd like to discuss your fault in detail,
press two for lies.

And judgements, ramifications Christian
dogmas and the control mechanisms operating on fear
hate and self-loathing.
Reactionary fundamentalists, I'm not sure are in tune
with reality, anything but. You can only laugh at 7000 years
and she said let's go scuba dive so we did
and as we get out of the water still screwing and bleeding
and my god those sharks where frenzied.
And imagine it, me out there like this
I don't do that
I never would
but I did.
We're gonna make this work for a while now that we are
enlightened and that now unblinded
we can better see all the lies about being free.
Since she got her engineering degree she walks tall not hunched
over like before, it was miraculous
it was just an inch but it felt like miles

Good times this week we are still reeking of sea water
and blood and sex and those sharks!
My god!
We came to quote somebody up in the White House
some fool talking all apologetic saying
I don't think that's gonna work for her new found confidence
chiming in like a bellowing from a dying horse.
We captured all the Arab areas
they are free, saturated under glossy propaganda and our dumb
excuses for democracy
till the chickens come to roost.
They lied and we knew it and no, complacency is complicity
you don't have to go on the spinach diet too.

That week we had chewed up what was left of our credibility
And ended a shaky relationship

It is seeming if you now know you
You know you're on the right track finding a story that fits your
needs if it makes you very uncomfortable it means now you are free.
We came together surrounding the hardest choices and as a
nation We failed miserably, literally overnight we fucked up everything even our own economy.
I woke up and instead of having to be somewhere I just lay there
maybe fall back asleep.
And as the military regularly on patrol are guarding our borders
they had electric eyes installed everywhere.
We flew right through at like 640 miles an hour with not even a peep
Yes its dangerous but that's what presents us as divine
dangerous, invisible and yes free

August was signing on for Wall Street deregulation now
that's a present to all the edifices built to celebrate injustice
oligarchodemocracy and neo-liberal policies, libertarian
then decided to do airstrikes against that strange relationship
with the Saudi sheiks and guillotines
10 k dead lives in very different places
if it's true they will stand behind you but if you disagree they
break out tanks tear gas rubber bullets swat teams
just sing a song about the killing of cops and watch
they walk with no accountability
on a tall pretty opening the crowd hands in the air gassed
guns that have been fired for freedom of speech
it's to show for us what is really up their sleeve
we saw it quoted in guttural throated screams
hands up coughing
freedom
it's tear gas mixed in
a terribly pretty large open door with noxious odors
and violent police
and I ran, we all ran as the brutality came down on us
bleeding in the streets

as tears rained down from our statue miss liberty who had
no shoes on

I was kind of staggering I was feeling weak
I had no wallet so you know how it is to feel the violence of
poverty and its malnutrition and hunger and how it makes for
bad tempers and pettiness very bad days and shitty forms of
exhaustion and torturous forms of trickle and vicious forms
of need when the US military guys stand up as they did that
man driving up half blind couldn't see so there he was prostrate
in a pool of blood another black man dead another shot down
like a dog with rabies a bullet to the head.

I feel maybe it's time to get packing
and I was like no I'm out of here
I scrape my windshield and clear out my shed behind a
cabana and you left this paper there of things unsaid
we can say this now scream it loud—
Its gonna be a long term of struggle
enjoying the absent control as riots
break out and society breaks down can we unite to fight
I am going to join you as we need to set aside all that petty
constructed BS built up to divide us.
Those hours I knew coming quick
I'd have freedom if we can hold hands, pick up your human
brother 'cause color doesn't matter anymore.
Hands in her face wiping away mace, tears fall like rain
as her eyes burn from toxic waste she composes herself, she
gets closer to those that before she was afraid.

United they rise up together, make change covering the
regions with direct action and non-violent rage—he's there
To cover the war for the New York Times In these days even
the press is not safe so stand up from the back in the front again
deep deep pull it out now the justice is fake put it together

now cause now you know how dirty they play and how your
false flag freedom is rigged and the market is played.
Time to unite
Time to resist
Take back our ideas and bring back the ringing bells of
fairness of play and justice, and freedom and the
dawning of a new day.

In Paris
by John Peterson

Oh Toulouse we did it—at the Moulin Rouge
We, you and me and these girls and guys
We danced the way a baby dances, free and easy
You with your short legs dance with them
Me with my cane dances with them
Kiirsti in all her glory dances with them

They sang, we clapped and the body imagined
Showed us the most daring moves

And today with Kiirsti
And my brothers and sisters
From another life
The portals opened by brush and paint
And yes all of us here in communion
With your world

And you there August
in the garden café and the dancing and laughing
and sweetness of night, the girls and their
luminous faces arising out of many
gone days, alive in the eternity we share
Your brush and your eye, your
willingness and ours to make it
again and again

in beauty   it is done
in truth   it is done
in love   it is done

yours, theirs, mine and ours
we do it because it is done by us

my friend   August Renoir

My Love for You
by Lisa Watkins

My Love for you will
never stop/end!
My love is like the never-ending
shine from the sun that
spreads as far as it can around
the earth. The shine from the
brightest clouds that show our
happiness for one-another, the
rain and lightning as protection
from any hindrance that
comes our way.
My Love for you will
never end!

Beauty in Brokeness

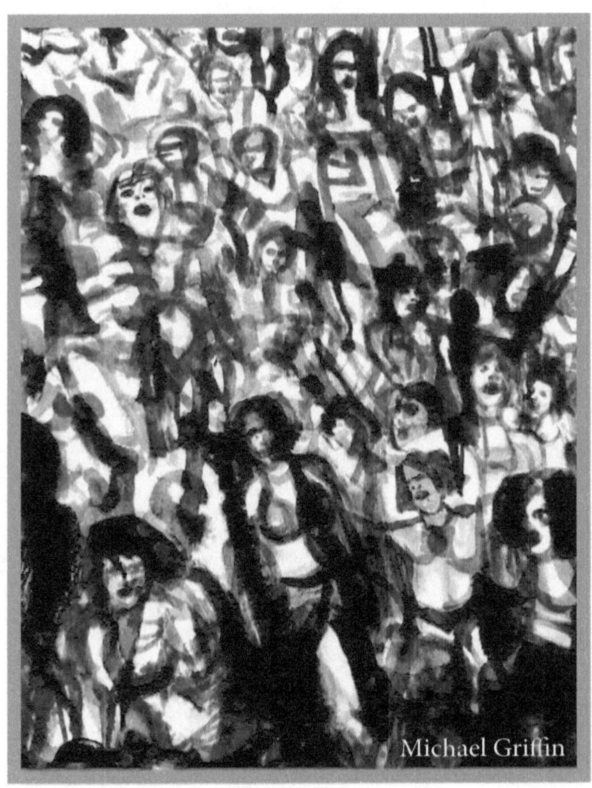

THE BEAUTY IN BROKENESS
by Amanda Raymond

How can you outpour love, grace, and joy
When you are filled with pain, fear, and anger?
How long can you take it?
How long must you fake it?
There is chaos in my stillness
There is screaming in my silence
This vessel is cracking
I've been told buried memories never die
It's true
They grow roots deep inside of you
They alter who you are
They suffocate the truth—
The truth of good…
The truth of bad
The roots grow deep
They create a hole
When the hole can get no deeper,
the roots spread
They grow outward
They grow upward
They invade
They infect
They take over
They attach themselves to whatever they can
They shoot off tiny tendrils to consume the smaller spaces
I prune the roots as they become exposed outside of my vessel

Seems that pruning makes them more resilient
This vessel's cracks continue
I feel it in my body
I see it when I look in the mirror
It won't be long until it breaks
With parched soil pouring out
Then what?
I've been told to surrender it to Him
I've been told in all things trust Him
I've been told He's making me new
I've been told there's beauty in brokeness

ONESELF
by Lisa Watkins

I am oneself
I wouldn't change oneself for nothing
oneself is in charge of oneself
oneself knows their choices, decisions
and nobody can help oneself only oneself can do it
One self can only allow things to be done or affected
one's self is very talented sweet caring
Oneself can improve its oneself when it wants
oneself always prepares for anything or things happening
one self doesn't care for trouble ordinarily
oneself can only be oneself
Oneself is very funny and can have lots of fun
but only oneself can do that, can you figure it out
what I'm talking about there can't be any confusion
About one self
you can't hide oneself either
oneself is always there you can't run from oneself either
you have no choice but to love oneself
You've got to love oneself
oneself love
To be happy

A Little Old and Bent
by Randy Hayes

He's a little old.
And a little bent.
To those in need.
He's heaven sent.

Up every day.
At the crack of dawn.
He just keeps right on.
A carryin' on.

I saw him up.
And out this morn.
Heavy coat.
And work boot shorn.

In his truck.
To warm it up.
In his hand.
A coffee cup.

Truck bed full.
Of his working tools.
This man plays.
By his own rules.

Foot on the gas.
And away he goes.
He's a workin' man.
As everyone knows.

GOD'S IMAGE IS GOD
by John Peterson

After listening to Allen Watts
Speaking of how Hindu's greet
everyone as God
And how the Hebrew God created
man/woman in his image
and we are made of the stuff of the universe
And so if God's image is God so we are created

I sit at the Tony Bennett concert
and look out at all us gods and goddesses
And it is a wonder   so many shapes
and sizes as is God's disposition
We are young and old   worn and carefree
We gods are all of it and we nod to each other
and go about that which is us
Tony does what is his perfection and I am grateful
I go about mine   and on and on and on

We are not through yet
The age cycles
as simple as the day
But we are still in an early hour
As Siddharth came to toil an hour for all time
Our time is yet
As Jesus was the sun of an age and answered a question
Our age has hosts on the precipice
The unveiling is still to come
And we are ready as some prepare
the other regions and some this
The cycle comes small and large
no matter our desire

THAT SCREAMING CAR NOISE
by Gary John Amstutz

You came into my life with pain
You torment me; make me insane
Each time I start my little car
You scream at me; from near and far

What once was such a quiet car
Now screams like beasts trapped in a jar
We changed the fan, the shroud, the belts,
Fluid, sensor, all quite expensive
Searching, Searching, Searching, Searching
The quest for truth was quite extensive

Thousands! Thousands! you must spend
The search for truth will never end
Fix it here; fix it there;
Fix the systems everywhere!

You guys have lost your frigging minds
Take all my cash and waste my time
I'm leaving now I'm off to find
Someone who'll fix this car of mine

Meanwhile good folks around me stare
Each time I drive; if I dare
So cringe; so loud; sounds cheap, and creepy
The mystery noise would not be sleepy

Rejoice! One day I find the minds
Who right away knew how to find
The truth, the cure, once more, this time
Brought back the quiet; my peace of mind

Those guys were treating you like a chump!
You only need a water pump!

Thank you smart guys fast and kind
Fixed this wonder car of mine
Saved the day, once more, this time
Until the next noise blows my mind

(End of part one Season 1
20 Seasons available)

OUR DREAMS
by James Taylor

Some dreams fall to the floor and break
They lie broken and shattered
Beyond repair

Some float around in the air
Seeking direction
while others slowly float away
out of reach and gone forever

there may be plenty left in your pockets
you may need deep pockets
to keep them going
it's up to you to keep your dreams alive

they are a small living entity
that can mushroom beyond expectations
as the doubters watch them blossom
like an optimistic flower looking for the grand sky

they may drift up to that telephone pole
landing next to roosting pigeons
the pigeons will peck away at them
as you watch them turn into particles
carried away on the wind

perhaps they will land under a young tree
like sprinkled fertilizer to be a nourishing inspiration

Finding The Music
by Michael Schulte

Song is missed
Slipped my grasp
Belonged to me
But not without you.

I might invite
all the spirits
to unite
under the umbrella
of my dreams.

Finding spaces in the traces
on the sheets of paper
the faces
of the ghosts
haunt me

Lay out my arms
Prostrate my soul
into the psalms of my hands
I find the song.

DREAMERS
by Randy Hayes

Dreamers dream.
And pine away.
For what they've lost.
From yesterday.

Long lost loves.
Or places gone.
An empty bed.
Early dawn.

Children grow.
And move away.
Old hearts break.
In their own way.

Hands and arms.
Empty grow.
We still can dream.
And feelings show.

When we dream.
In the night?
Our hearts show.
Great insight.

But those that dream.
In the day.
Pick the good.
Chase bad away.

BATTLES
by Vincent Carmack (8 years old)

There are so many battles
fire and ice,
sand and wind,
water and earth,
there are so many battles
that you wish you could declare.

Rise of the Dinosaurs
by Vincent Carmack (8 years old)

When the volcanoes rose,
  and the dinosaurs went down
  Only one survived like the Yoshi's round
  Nobody knows if a dinosaur would live to see today
  scientists are still trying
to make some come back to life
from their frozen form
  people really do not know
what some dinosaurs really looked like
  they always go by the bones
but that cannot stop us
  as long as we believe in ourselves
true stuff will be written.

GROWING OLD
by Christopher Buffalo Folsom

When I was young I was strong and sure
And felt this state would forever endure,
Although it did persist and hold,
And made me confident and in control,
Carrying beyond most others realities,
Eventual decline, to my Surprise,
now has hold of me!

Boots
by Mara Heller

A mass of emerald and ocher leaves,
sway upon the light summer breeze.

Suction of boots too big, wrenched from the muck,
grunting, banging, the metal bucket thunks.

The old farmer in his coveralls stands at the fence,
watching the struggling girl, as buckets bang, eyes wince.

'Ya wanna ta' feed um' he urges her on,
huffing, puffing, nose wrinkled of odors not fond.

A glorious glint of green and blue plumage,
is all that's needed to encourage.

Shrieking cries they emit, she jumps in fright,
screaming, slipping, sliding, then caught in plight.

Stuck in the mud, smelling quite rotten,
are boots too big, long forgotten.

(This is a poem I wrote from the KRVAA poetry workshops.)

LOST AMONG THE CROWD
by Mara Heller

Pale, pink and alabaster blanket the earth,
a covering of delicate, velvet snow,
scattered under a labyrinth of darkened limbs,
visible by lantern lights and lunar glow.

With twilight eyes, watching them fall and sway,
the crisp flow of air, they writhe, flitter,
dancing to a haunting tune,
of a midnight Zither.

A single blossom struggles, breaks free,
swaying upon a dark wind of night.
Entranced by it's journey,
breezes sending it off in flight.

Gusts swirl a mass,
a tornado of pinks over the floor
lost ones, siblings, a swelling crowd,
all will be withered, no more.

Blossoms swirled, began to sink,
a fleeting, memory made.
Strings lament, a twang in the night,
song plucked, emotions cascade.

This frail moment,
abruptly lived, found.
The beauty of one, lost among the crowd,
blending in, amongst what litters the ground.

An Emerald Sea
by Mara Heller

Among gold-tipped, emerald waves of grass one can see,
an old, twisted, gnarled, hollow, solitary tree.

Splintered and broken, it grows no more,
limbs and bark remain on the surrounding floor.

Thin, gyrating, pleading branches reach and shout,
towards a sapphire sky, as whipped cream clouds drift about.

Gray and black the wood, dry, crumbling, rough to the touch,
it's been that way for some time now, as no one goes there much.

It's striking appearance implies a message of lost strength announced,
if it remains is unknown but it's visage is easy to recount.

Not sure why this tree has made an imprint on my memory, yet,
I can still feel the cool wind as I gaze upon it, in that vast emerald sea.

Run to Remember

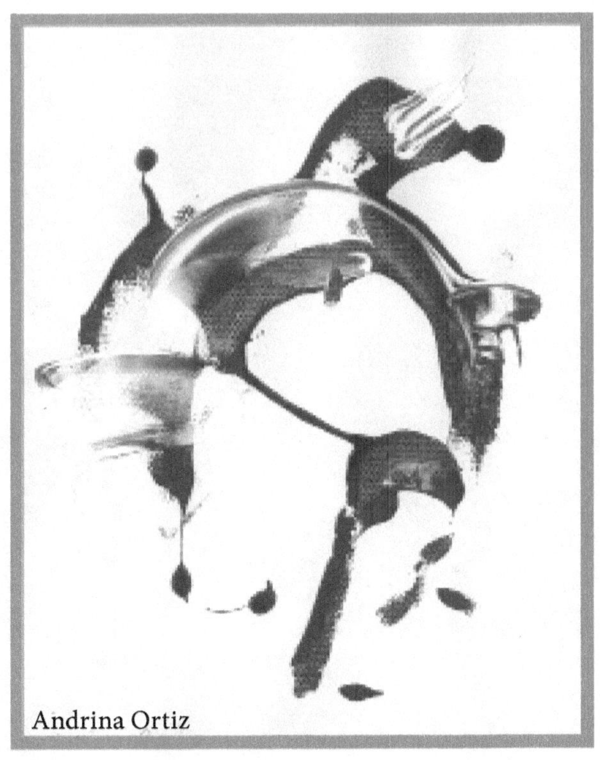

Andrina Ortiz

RUN TO REMEMBER
A found poem based on "Badwater" by Brent Puniwai

Nearly everybody said
that all those long lonely runs
under the harsh desert sun
had baked his brain.
But, one thing was for certain,
the Prince of the Sands was about to
run the race of his life.

ESPN never covered the race from a blimp.
Matter of fact,
they've never even covered the race.
Probably never will.

Exhaustion and the desert heat
can play tricks on a mind
and by the end of this race
most of the runners will have
given ESPN an interview
somewhere along the course
or somewhere in their minds.
I'd like to say that Sam was no different,
but he was.

You see, Sam ran to remember.
Anything could send him down that tricky path.
Like the lettering on the door of the truck,
The race stirred an avalanche of memories in Sam—
Some parts were his,
Some from things he had heard
And some that his mind, well,
just filled in the gaps…

The Farewell
by Doug Schanzenbach

A coopers hawk visited
Our bird bath today.
Perched on a center rock
Our house and hillside to survey.
We got out the binoculars
For a closer peek,
We scanned and examined
Feathers and beak.

He stayed a long time it seemed,
And left at the telephone ring.
The call was from the son of a
Dear ninety-year-old friend.
Thirty minutes ago his dad died,
About the time the hawk arrived.

My Grandmother
by Elizabeth Cards

My grandmother had a ring on every finger,
Which marked the passage of time.
Like a girl scout badge earned by being married to a man
That if he didn't drink had the shakes .
And, she held fragile family get togethers
covered by a veneer of being okay?
At the edge of constant threat of combustion.
Did love ever live there? Between the fingers of her despair?

"Why"
by Bill Hogarth

Why can't beautiful people slip easily from this life?
Why must the days, in so many ways, strain the love
between husband and wife?

Why can't the joys that are priceless and free
be appreciated more by us all?
And why can't life bring, with its promise of spring,
the fulfillment of dreams in the fall?

Why do we seldom help our fellow man as he
struggles along life's road?
Why do we ever so rarely assist those who carry
life's heaviest load?

I don't know the answers; I doubt that you do;
but I have to believe in God's plan;
He intended us all to give praise for our blessings;
and reach out to our fellow man.

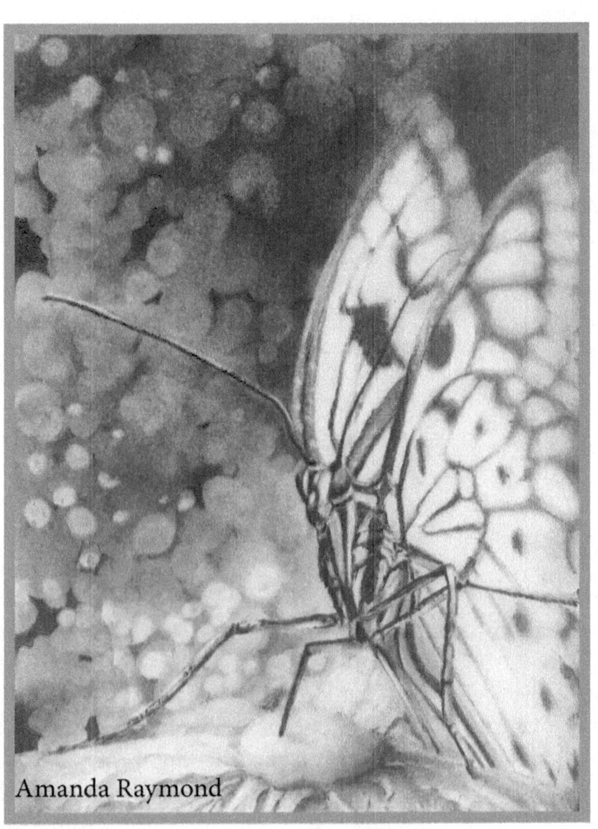
Amanda Raymond

On War
by Avraham Baruch Goldshtein

Loud booms all around,
Trigger at my hand and I,
Think I better run.

(This) is a haiku I wrote back in 2009, while deployed in Kosovo with
the US Army. Although I wrote it that long ago, it has remained one of
my favorite pieces due to its personal relevance. When I wrote it I was
in a "zone of imminent danger." But, more recently, during 2021, 2022
and even as close as a couple months ago, during the summer/autumn
of 2023, I've traveled extensively in Israel and the Ukraine, which have
been at war for some time now. Thanks to my constant thinking of this
little piece I've reminded myself that, sometimes, running is the
best form of defense.

Retrospect
by Chris Buffalo Folsom

As I live longer knowing that my life gets shorter
I live in wonder at the little things
Like stars and sunrise and
True friends and loves that
I wish I had met sooner knowing that
Now is the perfect time for
Everything!

Said I
by Avraham Baruch Goldshtein

Said I;
Having said nothing at all.
Said I,
Come tell, what of ye knoweth null,
But a speckle of truth,
Hidden yet of this 'ere cull,
Of this and that,
And nothing mor',
Over the land and o'er seas,
Seven, Said I,
O sir, indeed.

For knoweth I,
For knoweth thee.
O knoweth we,
Speckled, spackled truth and sea.

Wet ye're now,
Upon the tower,
And upon the heart of yonder 'ear,
Upon the days of yester;
A morrow and a day,
A night gone its way.

Ye're wet now,
But not before.
The sea takes hours,
And ye're no more.
Crazed young one,
You'll pay your wont.

Your desire;
Said I,
Will be your tomb awhile.

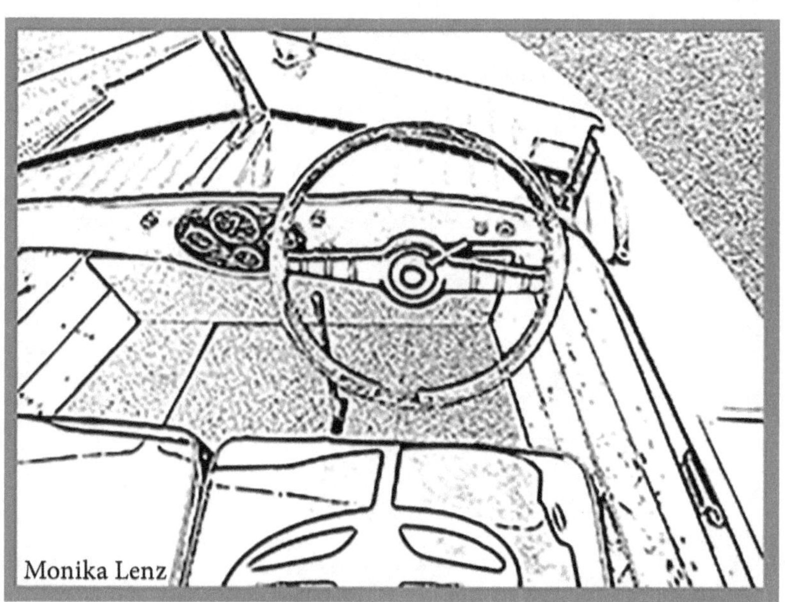
Monika Lenz

JOHNNY
by Monika Lenz

Johnny bought a Chris~Craft
          to cruise his blues away
He moored her near an old sloop
          down on Montego Bay

He polished her, he primped her,
          he sat on her deck each day,
he sang his boat to sleep each night
          down on Montego Bay

A storm came out of the south seas
          a hurricane they say
blew Johnny in his Chris~Craft
          out of Montego Bay

It tossed them, it turned them,
          it carried them away
It blew them out to the deep seas
          just off Montego Bay

Now Johnny has no Chris~Craft
          in a rubber raft astray
riding ten foot waves is he
          just off Montego Bay

Old Johnny had the blues once
          now he's washing them away
he's rotting in his rubber raft
          just off Montego Bay

Just To Lay Me Down Forever
by Magan Weid

Winding along my quiet route 'neath a roof of green trees,
Cedars and sequoias give way to the charm of broad leaves.
Knee deep, I push through thick seas of grass without end,
Until cool water sings to me, touches gentle my hand.
I sometimes long just to lay me down forever
Next to the bones of the river.

When the noise of summer is loud with all manner of things;
Guttural frog's moans and the droning buzz of insect wings,
And bugs that sing with the rub of their combed legs 'midst the smell
Of seeded stems and prickly vines, hummin' a witch's spell,
I'm oft tempted just to lay me down forever
Next to the bones of the river.

When the wind swings the leaves back and forth 'til the last let go,
Spinning them high or low, whatever way decides to blow.
Once-lively bushes have settled in for winter,
Frost begins to form and rocks begin to splinter.
'Side bitter water, I'll just lay me down forever
Next to the bones of the river.

When stars in icy air shine their brilliance all the brighter,
When day slumbers in layers, pulling its blankets tighter.
Memories grow weary of hidden hollows underfoot.
Snowflakes whisper drowsy lullabies everywhere I look.
'Neath frozen crusts, I'll just lay me down forever
Next to the bones of the river.

When blue mornings wake to the hurry of spring's long melt,
Huge, mossy stumps of ancient forests ring with songs heartfelt,
Darting twitters among heavy vines of rosebud displays
Lure caterpillars and gnats and all that winter delays,
Here I'll stay, night and day, once I lay me down forever
Next to the bones of the river.

The Road Less Traveled
by Randy Hayes

As for me?
I'll take the road less traveled.
The unmolested one.
The one not unraveled.

To wave at those.
On rustic porch.
Lighted by.
An old coal torch.

Where old cars sit.
On cinder blocks.
Guarded by.
Crows and hawks.

Where kids play.
In big mud holes.
Down by the creek.
With fishing poles.

Where skies are blue.
Not grey with smog.
Where people love.
Their scruffy dog.

Where barn cats.
Hunt rats and mice.
Where old folks.
Offer sage advice.

Where swings hang.
Over streams.
And fishes jump.
In young men's dreams.

Where they still read.
Twain's Huck Fin.
And they're happier.
Than, I've ever been.

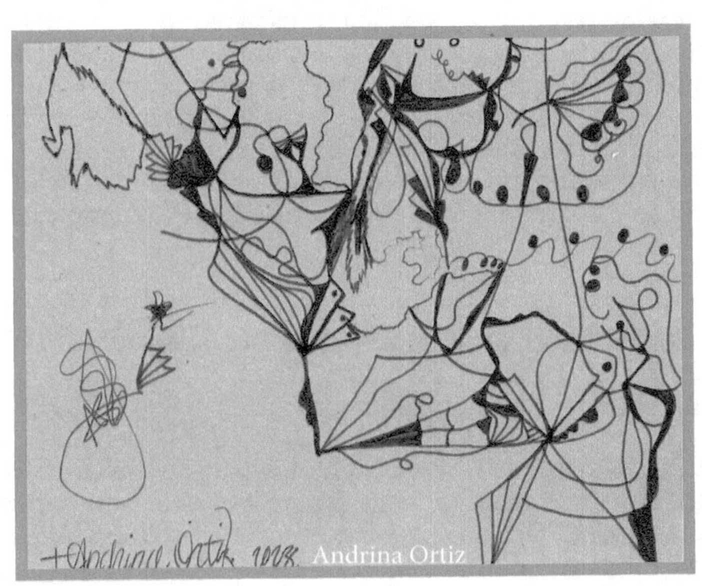

Andrina Ortiz

Gary Amstutz

Born in Toledo, Ohio where I studied Engineering Technology, began a career in Telecommunications, and escaped to Denver, Colorado and Boulder, Colorado for 5 years at Nortel Networks accepting promotions with ever increasing responsibilities then transferred to California with Regional Engineering responsibilities then later transferred to a branch as Consulting Systems Engineer for 7 more years. Next worked at GTE (which became Verizon Communications) for 10 years as a Sales Engineer then retired. Proud father of Julia Amstutz who is finishing her bachelor's degree at Cal State Northridge in Cinematic Arts.

Donna Miranda-Begay

Donna Miranda-Begay is former Tribal Chairwoman for the Tubatulabals of Kern Valley. Her Tribal affiliation is Tubatulabal, Paiute, Tule River Yokut, and Dine'. She is founder of the new non-profit California Tribal GIS. Her vision for CA Tribal GIS is assist CA Native American Tribes with GIS (mapping technology) knowledge build to assist with protection of cultural landscape and natural resources management. Donna enjoys creating and teaching both hand-made and digital Native American cultural art, writing poems, researching her Tribal history, creating traditional Tribal music and cultural site monitoring.

Vincent Carmack

Vincent discovered he enjoyed poetry while attending a poetry reading with his mom when he was seven years old. He loves all things Snoopy, going camping, and traveling with his parents. He wants to be a paleontologist when he grows up.

Joan Desmond

Joan Desmond is a visual artist and poet living locally. "My writing and art often reflect my interactions with the natural world." joandesmondwordpress.com

Chris Buffalo Folsom
  Sculptor, writer and President Kern River Valley Art Association.

Avraham Baruch Goldshtein (preferred nom de plume)
  Born in the heart of Mexico's Capital City, Avraham Baruch has traveled the world extensively; stopping by great cities and shanty-towns all the same and living through a myriad of exciting days and nights, some with friends and family, some others utterly alone in many middle-of-no-wheres yet unknown to man. Living now in the Kern River Valley, Avraham Baruch hopes to find the other side of things, where thought encounters fact, yet nothing is settled down. Not just yet at least.

Chris Gafford
  Chris is an artist who spends time between the Kern River Valley and Ridgcrest.

Michael Griffin
  Living in the Kern River Valley.

Mara Heller
  Mara is an avid reader/writer who also enjoys silver smithing and making jewelry. She also enjoys traveling or flying kites with her husband and son.

Bill Hogarth
  I am 89 years young; have been writing poetry since my teens. Never published (but occasionally included in local papers} since moving to Kern Valley in 1980.
  As a teenager, I sang "The Blind Ploughman" by Vincent Yeomans at Syracuse University in state finals, so my attentions are often drawn to religious expression.

Randy Hayes
  My name is Randy Hayes. A California native, born in Oxnard and raised in Ventura county. I started writing poetry when I was about 15 years old. I'm 71 at this time. And I enjoy writing about whatever comes to mind.

Sandra Rose Hughes

Sandra is a mother of five beautiful children and one rather irritating cat. She spent six years teaching English at Kern Valley High School and retired twelve years ago to become a stay-at-home-mom/writer. She is an active member of Mt. View Baptist Church of Lake Isabella and she loves poetry because she believes it can help heal the soul.

Monika Lenz

Monika lives in Lake Isabella with her husband Karl Olmstead and four dogs.

Andrina Ortiz

Artist in the Kern River Valley.

Brent Puniwai

Brent passed away Thursday afternoon, January18, 2024 after a brief battle with Cancer. There are no words to describe the loss to us all, especially the Kern River Valley Art Association.

Brent walked into the Gallery during a Board Meeting the very first Month we were open at 6749 Wofford Blvd. Although there were many who did not believe we could create the Gallery, he immediately supported and understood our vision becoming an integral part of our team…

Brent was an amazing graphic and all around artist… He was a gentle giant of a man and loved donning his Bigfoot outfit and doing short Squatch films where he would give advice. He was soft spoken and thoughtful and helped me make hard decisions. And his sense of humor always made me smile. His is a void that cannot be filled! …Thank you my friend for all that you gave us! We all love you!" (tribute written by Christopher Buffalo Folsom)

John Peterson

John created Poetic Matrix Press with James Downs in 1997. We have publisher over 100 books, primarily of poetry, since then. John has published 5 poetry books including: *Amtrak Starbucks Jazz on the Streets of Richmond; The Nature of Mountains; News of the Day; dark hills and wild mountains* and *Two Races One Face Two Faces One*

Race with Tomás Gayton. He has most recently published *Exploring the Poetic Matrix - Musings on Us and the Planet and How we are in the World,* a book of essays and poetry.

Amanda Raymond

Hi. My name is Amanda Raymond. I have been living in the Kern River Valley for 12 years to date. I have enjoyed writing of all forms since childhood, but creative writing, prose, and poetry have been a form of therapy for me. Thank you for taking the time to read my work.

Kimberly Salazar

"Kimberly's hope is that you can SEE situations in which other beings need help and (like a superhero) choose to take matters into your own hands to fix it. Its the small acts of kindness that return light, goodness, and hope to the world… it only takes a small flame to light the next candle and to put an end to the dark."

Michael Schulte

Like the guy at the AM/PM, Michael is an erudite space turtle with an ability to stop time and make time for others. Nothing more about him matters than that he tilts at windmills, and yet still has managed in this life to find his best friend from all his prior lives—Margarett.

Doug Schanzenbach

Doug is a Vietnam United States Marine Corps. veteran. A graduate of University of South Dakota with a BA in Government and The American University in Washington, DC with a MA in Management Systems. He is the author of the poetry book entitled, "Vietnam: My Long Journey Home." The father of three and grandfather of thirteen, he has been married to wife Elizabeth for the past 17 years.

Catherine Stachowiak

Catherine Stachowiak's poetry appeared in Los Angeles County wide anthology in the late 1970s. Since then

her poetry was published in many publications including
the Simi Valley literary journal "Verve" and ArtLife Limited
Editions, which was collected at renowned museums
including The Getty, New York Metropolitan Museum
of Modern Art, the Boston Museum of Fine Art and in
archives, museums and libraries throughout the United
States, Europe and Japan and once was the best selling
periodical at the Guggenheim Museum bookstore in Soho,
New York. She also worked as a journalist for the Sespe Sun,
the Fillmore Gazette and the Kern Valley Sun.

James Taylor
        I'm an artist working in watercolor and I also enjoy
drawing. I also do some very basic digital work. I also enjoy
writing poetry. I love when the thoughts and words appear
out of nowhere with wonderful spontaneity. Painting and
poetry are great companions. I often write a poem inspired
by a painting.

Lisa Watkin
        Lisa lives in Bodfish with Jason.

Magan Weid
        A part-time poet who has made KRV my full-time
home for a few decades. It's the perfect place to be inspired
by wonder and beauty, in both nature and the vast wealth of
vibrant creativity in the wonderful people who surround me.

Note your favorite pieces. Write your response to a piece. Write your own poem; to your lover, to the land, to your spiritual source, to the life that is gifted to us all. Enjoy!